VERNACULAR HISTORY SERIES

ALL THIS AND NO N

CW00798713

VERNACULAR HISTORY SERIES

The 'Vernacular History' series of books and booklets, of which this is number two (although the first published) gives a picture of life 'as it really was'—or at least as it seemed to be to those living it at the time: and the time may be as early as the first decade of the twentieth century, or possibly even earlier, up to the quite recent past. There is no precise time of 'cut-off' and the intention of the series is to show life as it was experienced by those involved—and perhaps to correct impressions given by fictional events in a fictional landscape. The series is similar to the **Life in Lincolnshire** series except that the scene is not necessarily restricted to a Lincolnshire setting and, in general, the books are likely to be considerably shorter.

These accounts may sometimes be the work of men and women experienced in writing but also they may sometimes be the work of those who have not had the benefits of extended formal education and have never previously written for publication. So far as practicable editing has been kept to a minimum with the account being presented in the words of the author and any illustration being from contemporary material. Although memories are not infallible, and some recollected detail may have become embroidered with the passage of time, the books are intended as factual records of the experiences of men and women, in all social groups, which might not otherwise have been preserved.

ALL THIS
— AND NO MILK
A TALE OF LIFE IN THE HOLBEACH MARSHES
1933-1935

by

Eli Hague

1970  1994

RICHARD KAY
80 Sleaford Road • Boston • Lincolnshire • PE21 8EU

© Eli Hague 1994
ISBN 0 902662 22 8

Typeset on an AppleMacintosh computer using Microsoft Word and PageMaker applications and reproduced initially by means of a LaserWriter Plus laserprinter.

Printed by The Echo Press, Jubilee Drive, Belton Park, LOUGHBOROUGH, Leicestershire. LE11 0XS

Contents

Leaving Home .... 7.

My New Home .... 12.

The People – First Impressions .... 14.

To Be A Farmer's Boy .... 16.

The Gentle Giants .... 32.

Sam's Tractor .... 34.

Transport .... 38.

Entertainment .... 43.

Chapel .... 46.

A Strange Meeting .... 51.

The Weaker Sex .... 54.

Children .... 56.

The Lighter Side .... 57.

Celebration .... 59.

Leaving .... 61.

Conclusion .... 63.

Illustrations

1. Holbeach St Mark's village – outline sketch map, 1933 .... 6.
2. The first field that I worked in at Willowtree .... 16.
3. Rogueing at Willowtree .... 16.
4. Implements on the farm .... 17.
5. 'Watch mi master's chits, Boy!' .... 18.
6. Tractor and binder working .... 21.
7. Horses being watered .... 27.
8. A waggoner with his team .... 29.
9. Two ploughing engines .... 33.
10. Sam's tractor .... 34.
11. St Mark's church .... 42.
12. The author on the chapel outing .... 48.
13. Chapel outing, 1933 .... 49.
14. . . . and some went into service .... 50.
15. The *Marytrue* .... 52.
16. 'Ha' you got enough paint, Porky?' .... 59.

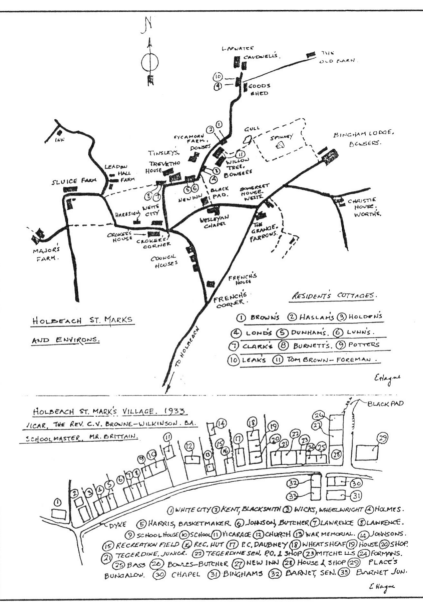

1. *Holbeach St. Mark's village 1933.*

LEAVING HOME

STALYBRIDGE, THE TOWN OF MY BIRTH, is a small town lying on the foothills of the Pennines some eight miles east of Manchester. In 1920 it was a busy, thriving centre of the cotton industry and few there were, from the cotton-masters to the millworkers, who could have forseen the dramatic changes that the next decade would bring.

By 1933, when I was 19 years of age, the Great Depression had reduced this once prosperous settlement to a virtual ghost town. The once noisy mills were silent and empty; the shops, one after another, deprived of trade, drew down their blinds and locked their doors and the growing army of unemployed, despair etched deep in their faces, shuffled slowly through the doors of the two 'unemployment' exchanges— one was a Mission Hall pressed into service because of the unprecedented numbers to be dealt with. And impotent fathers watched their children go hungry and their wives weep with despair.

It was in that year that I, an unemployed fitter and turner's apprentice, unwilling to wait Micawber-like for something to turn up in that dying town, bid my friends goodbye and set a south easterly course for the little village of Holbeach St. Marks deep in the flat marshlands of the Wash. I left no anxious parents behind; my mother had been dead some two years and shortly afterwards my father absconded for reasons which are beyond the scope of this book.

Now if inadvertantly it should be thought that my journey was a purely speculative one and I should be deserving of some credit for taking such a brave leap in the dark let me quickly correct the misapprehension. An uncle, one time native of my home town who had for many years lived and worked in the vicinity of St. Marks had made a visit to his mother and had also called on my father. I had heard him mentioned then that there was farm work available down his way for anyone who was not afraid of a bit of hard labour. I had learned my uncle's address at that time although not then thinking of leaving my home town. But the address stuck in my memory. Thus it was more than hope which sustained me during the eight days it took, by shank's pony and occasional lifts, to reach that remote rural outpost.

It was a chill grey morning in late March when at last I stood at the crossroads which marked the western end of that Lincolnshire village, The emotions that assailed me as I stood there were, I remember, a confused mixture of muted elation and apprehension.

Tramping alone and unaided across the width of England had been in the nature of an adventure; a journey from the known to the unknown. I felt justified in a little self congratulation but now that I was here what did the future hold? What sort of a fist would I make of this new way of life of which I knew nothing whatsoever?

But thankfully it is in the nature of youth to be blessed with a generous measure of resilience — both mental and physical. Slowly, almost imperceptibly my mood changed. Had I come thus far only now to give way to such pessimistic thoughts; to throw the towel in before the bell had even sounded for the first round?

In this more optimistic frame of mind I made my way along the village street — well rather more of a road than a street. My final destination did not lie here but a little distance away, and was to be reached by a route described to me in an earlier fortuitous meeting with a helpful local.

I still smile when recalling the circumstances of that meeting. As it had approached midnight on the previous day I had reluctantly come to regard as futile the possibility of reaching my uncle's home before he and his family had taken to their beds and seeing a convenient corn stack, burrowed a nest between the sheaves and slept there for the night.

A farm worker cycling placidly to his work the following morning had been half startled out of his wits on seeing a pair of legs emerging from the stack, but in the conversation which followed after he had regained his composure he imparted several items of information to me. Firstly it seemed I was lucky the rats hadn't 'had me'. Secondly he proved to be a workmate of my uncle and before mounting his cycle to resume his journey gave me precise instructions as to how my uncle's cottage could be reached.

The village was not as I had conceived it. No village green, duckpond or blacksmith plying his trade beneath a spreading chestnut met my gaze. Instead, almost all the buildings stretched in a line along one side of the road; a kind of pre-Victorian assay in ribbon development. The dyke which ran parallel to the opposite verge was probably the factor which had determined this unilateral disposition. The only exception to the general plan was a huddle of buildings at the top end of the road; these, consisting of two or three houses and a chapel, stood in the field beyond the dyke and were reached by means of a short bridge*.

My observations of the village were but superficial for, once again, I began to get butterflies in my stomach. Since I had only seen this relative of mine once before, and that when scarcely five years old, he could be regarded as falling into the category of a stranger. Now that I was only a mile or so from coming face to face with him my confidence began to ooze from my boots. Still, I put my best foot forward and proceeded on a search for The New Inn in the vicinity of which was the start of the Black Pad by which route I was to leave the village. Following this led to a road on which lay Willow Tree Farm. The cottage I sought stood but a few yards beyond this.

Scarcely half an hour later all my earlier misgivings, my niggling sensations of apprehension were wafted away like smoke in the wind. While still some fifty yards from my journey's end my uncle, having learned of my imminent arrival from his workmate, and consequently being on the look-out, came to meet me with the widest of welcoming grins on his

---

See the accompanying plan of the village – facing page 7.

weather-beaten face. The welcome was so warm, so genuine, that I felt overwhelmed.

Those next few minutes were a vaguely remembered blur of handshakes, introductions and eager questioning. When had I started out? Where had I slept ? Was I hungry? On receiving an affirmative answer to the last enquiry there ensued a quick foraging in the pantry and a rattle of pans.

That little cottage living room seemed crowded with folk. There was Sam, my uncle; his wife; their three daughters whose preparations for school had been interrupted by my arrival; and, in a pram, looking surprised by all the commotion, the youngest member of the family, a boy of two or three years of age.

It was the seductive aroma of frying bacon that reminded me that it was over a day since I had last eaten.

Some time after an ample breakfast had more than satisfied my hunger and the children with their lunch bags sent off to school I was first introduced to Mr. Tom Brown the farm foreman. Every locality has its 'characters'; Tom came into this category. No one could have imagined him— he had to be seen. Under the black, flat brimmed hat his lined brown face was embellished with a long straggly moustache which fluttered in the breeze like a bedraggled banner. A well-worn Norfolk jacket, knee breeches, buttoned-up leggings and ample sized boots completed the ensemble. Due to some past accident his left foot was turned out at a rather acute angle.

He could be dictatorial, peevish, placatory in a whining sort of way or downright obnoxious, all depending on whom he was dealing with. He had a predilection for addressing all males under the age of about twenty as 'little old boys'. Such was the individual who answered the Willow Tree farmhouse door in answer to Sam's knock. After a perfunctory handshake, a rather disparaging examination of my person – all five foot three of it – and a short sotto voce conversation between him and my uncle, it was arranged that I would see Mr. Brown at seven-o-clock the following morning in the stackyard when he would find something for me to do.

Nearly a full day to explore my new surroundings before being launched on my new career—so ran my thoughts as I headed back to the cottage which was to be my future home. The kindly, but the no nonsense housewife had other, more practical ideas. In almost no time at all she, the baby in the pram and myself were making briskly for the Post Office and stores of Mrs. Tegerdine in the village. There I was furnished with a pair of bluetts – they call them jeans to-day – a pair of stout boots, a collarless shirt of some thick woollen material, a pair of grey socks and a straw bass or bag for carrying my lunch. Payment it seemed would be made over the next few weeks out of my wages. On the way home it was explained that Mr. Haslam would lend me such essentials as spades, hoes and so forth until I could afford to purchase my own. Had I been their own son I could not have been the recipient of greater kindness and consideration.

My New Home

With my immediate needs catered for I could now take stock of the cottage in which I would henceforth live, and cast a more leisurely eye over a landscape so vastly different to that with which I had recently been familiar.

The cottage, set back from the road, was one of a pair—semi-detached the estate agent would call them. In the elevation away from the road a door led directly into the living room whose window overlooked a garden and the fields beyond. There was no front door. My recollections suggest that the room was somewhere in the region of ten to eleven feet square.

On the party wall, to the right as one entered, was the fireplace and chimney breast; in the right hand recess stood a coal-fired copper. The left hand wall was pierced by two doorways, one, nearest to the entrance, led to a moderately long but narrow wash house across the far end of which sat the sink furnished with a small hand pump. The water delivered by this was not suitable for drinking.

A larder lay beyond the second door. Water suitable for human consumption was stored there in two white enamel pails which were replenished as necessary from the pump in the front garden of the farmstead. In warm weather this water, unless freshly drawn was invariably tepid and not to my taste at all.

Since its confines were not intruded upon by either larder or wash room the front room beyond the far wall was much more commodious, providing ample room for the American organ which Sam had had transported from his parents' home some years previously.

I found three bedrooms in the upper storey. One led off to the left as you stood on the upper stair's landing; a second lay directly ahead and a third, smaller and more confined, could only be reached by passing through the second. This latter was the one in which I spent my nights.

Used as I had been to the amenities of the terraced houses of my home town it was novel to find a complete lack of gas, electricity or piped water. Lighting was by means of an oil lamp set in the centre of the table; cooking necessitated the use of the fire or a paraffin heated Dutch oven.

What increasingly surprised and intrigued me was the way in which the unflappable lady of the house contrived so effectively and efficiently the running of a household of seven people with only the aid of such basic amenities.

And what can I say of the terrain, the topography of that alien landscape as it appeared to me when I gazed upon it on the afternoon of that eventful day?

Standing on the road outside the cottage and scanning the scene spread before and around me I was filled with a sense of what I could only describe as unbelief. The flatness stretched on all sides as far as the eye could see; stretched and blended into the distant horizon so that the sky, except for the change of colour, appeared as an extension of the land. No familiar backcloth there of rolling moorlands or towering gritstone peaks.

No mills with tall, smoke plumed chimneys; no cobbled streets or corner shops; no cinema or billiard halls. But then neither were there knots of dispirited out-of-works or dole queues or pathetic people with little bundles waiting for the pawnbroker to open.

But there was a stillness, a brooding quiet unfamiliar to ears accustomed to the roar of mills, the rattle of tramcars, or the sound of steam trains drawing out of the local station. I missed for a while the melancholy train whistles in the night. Indeed for several weeks when I lay down on my bed at the end of the day this unusual lack of extraneous noises was largely instrumental in keeping me awake— ike missing an old familiar lullaby.

THE PEOPLE — FIRST IMPRESSIONS

THE AVERAGE TOWN OR CITY DWELLER is a rather insular individual. A busy thoroughfare may be alive with hurrying, introspective strangers who neither speak, unless directly questioned, nor expect to be spoken to. If asked they will proffer directions or the correct time of day; apart from that they pass each other by unnoticed and unnoticing.

How different, I found, were the inhabitants of St. Marks and its neighbourhood. As I wandered through the village, or walked along the roads which converged upon it, I was greeted almost without fail by every individual I encountered.

Labourers cycling to their work, women in the fields or those gathered around the Post Office called 'Good Day'. Most vociferous of all, groups of children bound for school waved and ventured an unabashed 'Hello'.

I said 'almost without fail'. There were those who weren't quite so 'forthcoming'; members of the opposite sex in those awkward in-between years—no longer children nor yet women. Those, either singly or in groups, approached me with averted gaze then burst out giggling once they had passed by. That was while I was still a comparative stranger.

Newcomers in a village community are usually objects of speculation and if their antecedents are unknown it may take some little time before they are 'accepted'. Living with my uncle who was a well known and respected resident and the church organist did much materially to shorten this acclimatisation period.

After this my new workmates did more than just bid me the time of day; their natural curiosity needed to be satisfied. Where had I come from and why? It was, to say the least, rather unusual to talk with people who had no first hand experience of the great depression, yet it was understandable, isolated as they were in those remote flatlands of the Wash.

Yet more surprising than that was the unexpected respect

they evinced for me when it was learned that I had been a regular supporter of Manchester United football club. On the merits of the various members of that famous club I was regarded as the unquestioned expert and was frequently called upon to settle their often acrimonious disputes.

To Be A Farmer's Boy

DURING THE FIRST YEAR of my emplyment at Willow Tree and Bingham Lodge farms there were scarcely any of the farm labouring activities in which I did not participate.

Never before in my life had I in any way been involved in gardening or the weeding of gardens; in the well remembered back streets where my boyhood had been spent there had been no gardens. My first job soon remedied this singular lack of horticultural experience; I was set to work hand-weeding several acres of William Copeland tulips. How my back ached at the end of that first day and with what relief I fell into my bed that night.

2. The first field that I worked in at Willow Tree Farm. William Copeland tulips which had to be hand-weeded.

3. Rogueing* at Willow Tree Farm.

* rogue, n. a plant that falls short of a standard, or is of a different type from the rest of the crop. v.t. to eliminate rogues from.

But thankfully I had not toiled alone; another newcomer had shared the seemingly endless day. He was a lugrubious youth of my own age whose six foot stature was crowned with an unruly mop of almost white hair. For more than half a century the friendship struck up between Fred (for such was his name) and myself in that field endured until his death earlier this year.

One morning some two or three days later the prevailing peace and quiet to which we had become accustomed was rudely disturbed by the sound of female voices; a gang of women and girls had arrived to pull the daffodils in the adjacent field.   Residents, mainly of Holbeach, they had travelled on a horse-drawn flat cart driven by the ganger, a certain Mr. Franks— the girls called him Franko.

They were a noisy, laughing, chattering group whose strident and often unladylike comments could be clearly heard the length of the field away. We sat with them in the lee of the fieldside hedge to eat our morning meal and I for one was struck by their frank and open manner. My strange northern dialect amused them but when they tried to mimic it I found myself laughing with them. I felt a little sorry when the field had been pillaged of its gold and they left.

Then there was the potato setting; another backaching job. The two of us,

4. *The 'ridger' in the foreground with, immediately behind it, 'an implement with conical studs'.*
(see next page)

Fred and I, bent double holding a chitting-box full of seed potatoes between us and dobbing them one at a time, into these little depressions. The ridger had drawn out the vee shaped grooves across the field and then an implement with conical studs projecting from the circumferene of its wheels had followed along— and that is how we got the depressions.

It was the chits of course which occasioned the greatest aggravation. Mr Tom Brown knew all about chits and insisted on imparting this knowledge to me— several times. He was never wholly convinced that without his constant surveillance a lad brought up in the shadow of mills and factories would remember, from one potato to the next, which way up they went.

Look back between my legs as often as I liked

5. *'Watch mi master's chits Boy!'*

and there would be that pair of acutely angled size twelve boots which told me a pair of untrusting eyes were watching my every move. He was paranoiac about those diminutive shoots.

Those days of moving across the seemingly endless fields with my nose never more than a foot above the ground effectively put paid to a cosy little theory that I had formulated; namely, that with practice I should happily become immune to backache and stiffness. I crawled home each night feeling worse than after those days of tulip weeding.

Bright-eyed, optimistic do-gooders seem to see it as one of their missions in life to cheer up all those who are not as cheerful nor free from care as they themselves. When happening across the despondent, the depressed, or even the desperate they have a trite saying, a kind of mental pick-me-up which asserts: 'Don't worry friend, when you are at the bottom there is only one way you can go—UP.' How I wish I could have met up with one or two of them after the day when, in company with the majority of the Willow Tree labourers, I ended my first day's stint of sugar beet singling. I would most cheerfully have strangled them.

'What do they know about "bottom"?' I growled to myself as I crawled wearily along that farm road in the gathering gloom with every muscle, every sinew, every bone crying out in protest. After potato setting I believed I had reached the bottom of the scale of pure, unimaginable physical distress; then it struck me forcibly that my own personal 'bottom' had lain a significant number of rungs lower.

The day had started out bright and fresh. Straws had been drawn to determine whose 'land' was which and then the work began. The idea was simple. With a short-handled hoe you chopped a gap in the row of plants with the intention of leaving but one. Failing this you grubbed out the redundant ones with your free hand. Bent double you thus chopped and singled as fast as you could moving sideways, crab fashion towards the distant headland.

When you contrived to stand erect for the purpose of taking a breather every part of your anatomy cried out in protest; and when it was desired to resume the former working position the same torture assailed you. Lest it be thought I exaggerate let me assure you that I observed seasoned labourers resorting either to the kneeling position or the use of the long handled hoe. This latter expedient evoked guffaws of derision from the more stoic and earned for them the demeaning title of 'old man.'

So stiff and incapacitated was I the next morning that I found it impossible to rise from my bed and my Uncle Sam had to drag me from beneath the sheets and help me to stand up and dress myself. As I ate my breakfast the prospects of yet another day of the same torment was almost unbearable.

An interesting sidelight on this business of beet singling concerned the village school. Mr. Brittain the headmaster was in the habit of sending out groups of boys under the control of a teacher for the purpose of measuring out such fields. From this information the areas of the 'lands' could be determined and, once the price per acre for the singling had been arrived at, the remuneration payable for each such 'land' could be accurately calculated.

One morning I walked into the stackyard to find I was to join a team of men who were preparing to go 'green taytn'. By this time the words 'tayts or tayuts' for potatoes were quite familiar to me— but 'green'? In answer to my question one of the men volunteered the information that it meant 'new'; mystery solved.

My knowledge of the local customs was further enhanced a little later when I observed with interest the ritual of bargaining.

While I, in common with the rest of my workmates sprawled on the side of the dyke outside the potato field, the ganger, a Mr. Bob French, and Mr. Tom Brown – sitting high in his pony trap – engaged in a heated discussion about the price to be paid for the work since it was to be carried out as piecework.

For reasons which I never fathomed out then, and still don't understand, it appeared that the tubers could be picked by the ton or by the acre and that a crucial factor in the decision was the size of the potatoes. When one insisted on a 'by the acre' arrangement the other was equally adamant on a 'by the ton' agreement.

To the best of my recollection negotiations broke down three or four times with Tom wheeling his trap round in the direction of Willow Tree at these junctures while Bob gathered us together with the terse instructions: 'Right men, let's go and try somewhere else.' But each time, as if by some traditional formula, Tom returned, we resumed our positions by the dyke and a fresh round of discussions took place.

Eventually when Tom had grudgingly raised his offer and Bob had reluctantly lowered his sights to a more realistic level a bargain was struck whereupon Tom rode off and the real business

20.

of the day began.

By this time, as a result of my previous labours in the fields, my muscles had become more inured to the physical exertions I was called upon to perform and I found scooping up the potatoes into a wire basket, running to tip them into the riddles in the centre of the field and sprinting back to my stretch, was a task I could perform as adeptly as most of the others.

Getting the best of our constantly grumbling foreman was a way of life on

6. Tractor and binder working at Holbeach Bank 1933/34.

Willow Tree. Be it besting him in a 'bargain' or contriving a brief spell of skiving with a Woodbine brightened the day no end. (Smoking was strictly forbidden within the farm boundaries.) Since neither Fred nor I smoked such a manner of scoring one over the old so-and-so was denied us but, surprising as it might seem, there was one memorable occasion when we confounded him in the matter of a 'bargain'.

One of the most arduous and unsavoury tasks that a farm worker could be asked to undertake was that of muck filling and my companion and I had been sent to the Bingham Lodge crewyards to do just that.

There was a brief haggling over the price. Tom, fully aware of our experience – or lack of it – both in farmwork in general and muck filling in particular, seemed unusually unconcerned when he heard our tentative offer. The twinkle in his eye and his ready, almost eager compliance indicated even to us his confident belief that we had grossly underestimated the magnitude of the task and would come out the losers by a considerable margin; I don't believe there was any inherent spite in his hopeful prognosis— it was just the name of the game.

Happily for us we had done our homework, questioning the last persons to do the job and ascertaining both the depth of the muck and the amount they had earned on that occasion. A simple measurement followed by a proportionate calculation had furnished the price we tendered.

Yet I believe we would have been struggling to make the job pay but for the astute Fred's brainwave. Acting on this we dispensed with the usual time-honoured methods and made use of a stack knife to slice the muck up into cart-width strips, roll them up like a carpet and with the aid of muck forks heave them into the cart. It was a doddle.

Having to pay us almost three weeks wages for less than a week's work wiped the smile off that moustache adorned face. Mind you he didn't give us the grand total all at once but split up into two weekly instalments. Perhaps he thought Mr. F. H. Bowser would be prompted to ask some awkward questions about his much vaunted 'bargaining' prowess. With some of that money I bought my first second hand bicycle.

Harvest time came and the binder, a mysterious contrivance which had long engaged my curiosity, was drawn out of the implement shed to be cleaned and oiled. Meanwhile a team of men armed with scythes set out for the first field to be cut.

Fortunately, as I saw it, Jennie, the wife of the redoubtable foreman had commandeered me to cycle to the village on an errand. Since the field in question was bordered by the road the temptation to see what these men's job was to be proved irresistible. I was glad I did so for I witnessed the practice of a rural craft which in a year or so would be seen no more.

They were 'opening up' the field so that the binder could 'set in' without running over and damaging the corn adjacent to the headlands. With smooth, seemingly effortless swinging strokes, they scythed a wide strip around the perimeter of the field.

From time to time they paused, and drawing a cylindrical carburundum stone from a waist pouch resharpened the arc-shaped blade before resuming their task.

Later in the day from an adjacent field in which I had been set to work it was possible to watch the horse drawn binder progress steadily round the standing corn; to see that corn being swept back onto the reciprocating mower blade by rotating arms; watch its progress up the conveyor to the rear of the machine and observe how it was bundled into sheaves, bound with binder twine, knotted and thrown onto the stubble.

The reasons for my non-participation in this harvesting of the corn were two fold. Firstly the Irishmen had arrived making the presence of one such as myself quite superfluous and secondly because the following morning Mr. F. H. Bowser, through the medium of Tom Brown, requested my immediate presence at Bingham Lodge.

Being sent for by the Master (so Tom always addressed him) was an event calculated to fill even the stoutest heart with a measure of apprehension. How I racked my brains trying to recollect what misdemeanour of mine might have occasioned his displeasure—there seemed no other reason for such a summons.

Thankfully no reprimand awaited me; instead, having learned of my previous occupation, the boss had decided I was just the person to sharpen the multi bladed cutters for the binder. How good it was to stand before a vice again with a file in my hand doing something in which I was trained and competent.

Earlier I mentioned the arrival of the Irishmen at Willow Tree. Seeing that I became quite friendly with these seasonal immigrants from across the water I feel justified in including them in these memoirs. Perhaps I was a little naïve, somewhat over sentimental; maybe as an immigrant myself a certain empathy coloured my emotions and reaction at that time. Whatever the cause I felt sorry for them.

Apart from those directly responsible for their temporary employment I found precious few who welcomed them. To a certain degree this antipathy was understandable. They came at the busiest time in the farming calender primarily to help with the harvest when most of the work was done by the 'piece'.

Locals had toiled through the comparitively lean times of winter and spring, often frozen by the piercing winter winds and soaked by rain. Sometimes, when the weather was unfavourable, some had been stood off with a corresponding loss of earnings. (Remember that farm labourers were not covered by the Unemployment Act — any reduction in the weekly wage of around 35/-, or £91 per annum, was a serious blow.) Of course those employees living in tied cottages benefitted from the relatively low rents but were well aware that loss of their job meant loss of tenure.

Harvest time provided the opportunity to earn that much-needed extra cash, especially in families with children to rear: and now came the Irish to skim the cream. This I feel was the main objection against the intrusion.

On the other hand there was a reasonable argument in favour of bringing in the additional labour force. The gathering of the harvest is not a factory style operation to be started or stopped at the dictates of the manager. Season and weather are beyond the control of man; nature stipulates the time when certain things must be done and it always seemed to me that without the aid of the transients it would have been difficult if not impossible to complete the work within the inflexible time scale thus ordained.

Apart from the rancour thus caused a certain amount of disquiet was sometimes expressed by parents, especially the mothers of young daughters. On more than one occasion I heard perfectly rational and unfanciful mothers of my acquaintance, on the occasion of their female offsprings leaving to visit relatives or attend some function in the village, admonish them with: 'And be sure you're home before dark and don't get talking to those Paddies.' The inference was painfully obvious.

Sure, Pat and Paddy liked their ale. More than once, cycling home in the dark hours, I came across a recumbent figure sprawled on the edge of the field besides the Black Pad but I never once heard of one of them being involved in anything even slightly questionable as a result of their inebriation.

What, I used to wonder, would the villagers have had them do after a hard day's graft; no cheerful fireside and homely comforts awaited them. Far from home and amid strangers, they often frequented the only place where it was warm and the company reasonably convivial. The landlords of the New Inn and the Wheatsheaf weren't about to turn away good customers.

My first real contact with them happened quite by chance. I was leaning against a corn rick in the stackyard one warm evening playing a tune or two on my mouth organ when one of them approached me. 'Do you know any of the songs of the Old Country?' he enquired. On my assuring him that indeed I did he asked if I would 'come up' and play some for him and his fellows. It never entered my mind to refuse.

So I climbed the steps leading to the loft above the stables where they were billeted. It was a bare, shadowy comfortless place inadequately illuminated by candles stuck in bottle necks. Around lay bags stuffed with straw— passable palliasses. It seems they had almost run out of funds so, clubbing together, had managed to furnish themselves with a solitary bottle of the 'hard stuff' – Irish of course – and were sitting in a circle passing it round from hand to hand. I declined their invitation to: 'Go on boyoh, just a nip.' During the course of that well remembered evening I played and they sang every Irish song I knew— and some I didn't until that night.

Then and on subsequent gatherings their leader and organiser acquainted me with the set up. He was responsible for recruiting them in their home country and shepherding them to Willow Tree. All money due to them was paid to him each week and from that he doled out a fixed amount of spending money to each individual; enough for a reasonable quantity of ale and the necessary incidental expenses they were likely to incur. The bulk of the money he saved, turning it over to them only when they had landed on the dock in Ireland. Otherwise, he confessed, there was every likelihood of them returning home as empty-handed as when they had set out. In addition he paid Jenny, the foreman's wife, for cooking their meals and providing any other necessary services.

There were some who viewed my fraternisation in a poor light but I chose to ignore them; as I said—I felt sorry for the Irish men.

Before that first year was out I had picked main-crop potatoes—King Edwards and Majestics; earthed up graves at three pence a yard (both sides inclusive); chopped sugar beet while protecting myself from the pouring rain with three sack bags, one wrapped around each leg and the other draped over my head and shoulders, and riddled potatoes with probably the best gang in the Marsh at that time. Now *that* was an achievement to be proud of.

During all this period on only one occasion was I entrusted with the handling of a horse; this was on the day Fred and I started our muck filling.

'Seein' as you're off to Bingham, boy,' said Tom, with one foot on the mounting step of his trap, 'take Bounce wi' you. He's in the top stall; you'll find his tackle on a nail 'side of the manger.' Then he was up and off.

Bounce was a black, sullen looking creature with big brooding glass-alley eyes; he towered over me like a haystack and introduced himself by trying to push me through the stall partition. He never took to me. Perhaps my failure to reverse the collar before trying to slop it over his ears riled him; there were certainly all the signs of marked disapproval in the way he raised his head, snorted and bared his yellow teeth.

26.

'Help you mister?' I hadn't noticed the chit of a lad who had followed me into the stables to watch my antics; he got no arguments from me. Reaching up he grabbed a handful of mane, yanked it down to the accompaniment of a few terse words of command, reversed the collar and settled it down round the beast's neck. The other items of equipment were slipped into place with an enviable and obviously practised adroitness.

'I'll lead him over to Bingham,' he said. Somewhat mollified I trudged behind pushing my cycle. After that the

7. Horses being watered. Note the waggoner's sideways seat.

distance between horses and myself could never be too great.

Mind you, as an interested spectator I admired horses; I admired the power their strongly muscled bodies could exert, and marvelled at the docility, obediance and sagacity they demonstated when handled by those men they acknowledged as master.

In 1933 there were horses to be seen on every hand. They were the chief motive power on those wide-spread, fertile lands. Cycle to Holbeach, Shep Whites, St. Matthews or down the Bank — cycle anywhere you chose and in field after field could be discerned the patient, plodding horses drawing ploughs or rollers or harrows or whatever other implement the season dictated. One could come across them pulling carts or hauling the great four-wheeled wagons en route for Holbeach or Spalding stations. Come weekends and they would gladden the eye as they frisked and cavorted in the grassy paddocks.

When first seen the Marsh ploughman's method of controlling his charges intrigued me greatly. The need to guide both the plough and the horses at the same time was a contingency which had induced that breed of men to dispense with the centuries old conventional reins and introduce a more practical method.

I remember the first time I watched a St. Mark's ploughman turning over the furrows with a two horse team. He made use of one rope or line which was attached to the bit of one of the horses which consequently was known as the line horse. One tug on this line directed the team in one direction; two tugs urged the opposite. If, during some particular manoeuvre both hands were required on the plough the use of the line was dispened with to be replaced by verbal instructions. The commands 'Heat' or 'Heat up', signalled one direction; 'Come here', the contrary.

Of necessity every farm in the area had its stables; Willow Tree and Bingham Lodge had each its own string of horses and the appropriate accommodation. Even the Crown Colony houses down the Holbeach Road, had, on each seperate plot,

8. A waggoner with his team of three horses—the lead horse is not shown. Note the upswept ends of the typical Lincolnshire waggon. The photograph was probably taken several years earlier than the events of this book.

provision for stabling one or two such essential animals.

These farm stables and their equine occupants were in charge of an employee known as a waggoner or horseman (I found these terms used more or less synonymously). A second Tom Brown – no relation to the foreman – who resided in the cottage adjoining ours held this important position at Willow Tree. It was an onerous and responsible undertaking. Not only was such a person concerned with the feeding, grooming and general well-being of his charges but was required to be skilled at all those farming operations which involved the use of horses.

His day commenced at the early hour of five-o'-clock or thereabouts. Before I had become used to this routine my morning slumbers were often disturbed by the sound of heavy boots tramping below my bedroom window, accompanied by the rattle of buckets. The first essentials were the feeding, watering, grooming and general examination. Some time after six-o'-clock he would return for breakfast. Finally he made his was back to the stables some time before the start of work at seven-o'-clock. Then, besides selecting and harnessing such horses as he required for his own use he would indicate which horse would be allotted to this or that man for certain other specified duties.

The waggoner did not work with his team until the normal knocking-off time. We worked until four thirty in the summer months and four-o'-clock in the winter; he could be seen unhitching his team somewhere around two-thirty. His non-possession of a watch would not interfere with this routine for at the habitual hour the horse would halt and refuse to move an inch further in any direction save that of the stables.

It is not to be thought that the man's actual working day was terminated at this juncture. He needed to be present at the stables to deal with the many tasks attendant upon the return of his and the other's horses to their stalls. Finally, later in the evening, he could be heard making his last visit of the day in order to put the animals to 'bed'.

Naturally much training was required to produce a competent waggoner; consequently the farmer would engage a youg man as a learner or apprentice to the incumbent. This newcomer invariably 'lived in' with the waggoner's family even though his home might be just a mile or so distant. Thus were the future horsemen nurtured in their craft.

Although 'living in' also implied 'sleeping in' as well, this did not preclude the tyro from returning to his family home in the evenings or at weekends. Providing he carried out such tasks as the waggoner deputed to him he would more usually eat his suppers with his kith and kin and at weekends enjoy home cooking when he joined them round the same table for Sunday dinner and tea. The Sabbath was also a time when he could worship in the village church or chapel if such was his inclination. As his skill and expertise grew with increasing age and experience he usually aquired the title of second horseman.

Thus, over fifty years ago, I was priviledged to live surrounded by those magnificent beasts of burden; saw them as indispensable partners in man's constant endeavour to turn the brown, bare earth into a burgeoning area of fruitfulness. Little did I know then that the sun, whose rise would herald the dawn of that new era when the internal combustion engine and implement mechanism would revolutionise farming, was not too far below Time's horizon.

Perhaps I was not observant enough to perceive the faint gleam in the sky which portended the imminence of that daybreak. Yet in retrospect I realise that all the signs were there for the wiser ones to ponder over. We at Willow Tree had our tractor which Sam had driven from the day of its introduction. The Caudwells had at least two and shortly after I arrived the splutter and roar of a new Fordson in one of the Trevethoe fields announced another threat to the horse's long supremacy. On an afternoon shortly after my first Christmas in the Marsh I joined a jostling, chattering, wondering crowd of men in the yard of Trevethoe farm to witness the sale of their stable of horses and equipment. Old men shook their heads and wondered what the world was coming to and prophesied that the new-fangled, noisy, smokey engines would never catch on— no, dang it boy! Never!

Neither they nor I realised what we were observing— the beginning of one of farming's most significant revolutions and the inevitable demise of the horse.

THE GENTLE GIANTS

ALTHOUGH THE INTERNAL COMBUSTION powered tractor eventually became the undisputed power unit on well nigh all farms there were other machines with which man had sought to replace the horse; by far the majority of these had been produced by firms based in the County of Lincolnshire itself. These were the steam traction engines.

What spendid, impressive entities they were; I almost believed they had a soul. Even today they will draw their admiring crowd of young and old unable to resist the unfathomable magic. I can never explain why the smell of steam and smoke and oil, the hiss of escaping steam and the powerful beat of the exhaust is so compelling.

In those far off days I saw them not as brightly polished, gleaming objects of owner pride or spectator envy but as indispensable farm auxiliaries. The yard at Willow Tree was never so full of activity as when the engine arrived hauling the threshing drum. The alignment of engine and drum in preparation for mounting the driving belt evoked memories of the great Northern Wakes Grounds. I admired then, as I had often done as a boy, the nonchalent skill of the drivers as they manipulated the ponderous machines into just the right position. And then in an incredibly short space of time the flywheel commenced its steady, tireless gyration.

The stack visibly shrank as sheaves were flung down into one end of the drum while straw tumbled from the opposite end and capacious sacks were filled with the golden grain. The yard seemed filled with men, the air with smoke, steam, and wind-borne straw and the ears with the engine beat and the ceaseless thrum of the threshing drum.

One day I was working over at Bingham Lodge when I saw my first steam cultivator at work. The steam traction engines built specifically for the job were positioned on opposite headlands and disposed sideways to the run of the plough.

9. Two ploughing engines, the first of which can be seen to be beautifully maintained. The photograph was taken by the author at ' a show'.

Slung beneath the engine frames were horizontal rope drums. Two wire ropes were secured fore and aft of the balanced plough, one rope being wound round one engine drum and the second round the opposing and opposite drum. When one drum was clutched in and hauling the other was letting out. Thus the plough was drawn across the field. For the return run the two drums exchanged roles.

The operation required a complement of four men and a youth; a man on each engine, a man on the plough, a gaffer and the youth as a general dog's-body, cook and messenger boy. While they were on the site they ate and slept in a large, dark green painted van.

SAM'S TRACTOR

EVERY ONE CALLED IT SAM'S TRACTOR. Since no-one else had ever driven it I suppose that, excepting Mr F. H. Bowser, no other could stake a stronger proprietorial claim than my uncle.

There wasn't a more cossetted piece of machinery to be found between Spalding and the Wash. Of all the things he held dear that International 10-20 came second only to his dear wife; and if anyone should know it was my long suffering self.

10. This was the tractor that Sam drove. Made by The International Harvester Co.
We called it simply an International.
The company is now The Case International Harvester Co.
The last of this model was made in 1939.

A month or so before my first Marsh Christmas I was sent to help my uncle with the tractor ploughing. I remember telling someone what a nice change it would be; no more knocking thistles down with a scythe in the grass paddock or digging twitch out on the headlands when, at that time of the year, there was little else to do; a real doddle in fact. But I never ventured that opinion to Sam who wasn't slow to express the opinion that I was most fortunate, as a newcomer, to land such a plum job and really owed a great debt of gratitude to the beneficent master of Bingham Lodge.

The belief that I had landed on my feet proved to be correct—literally. There was to be no riding on the plough lest such thoughtlessness imposed an unwarranted strain on my mentor's well-nigh revered engine. Thus began my long saga of pedestrianism. Long miles of stumbling, lurching and tripping over fallen clods in the foot deep furrow as I followed the plough.

The tractor unfortunately lacked the recently introduced power take-off which mechanically expedited the manipulation of such implements as were being hauled behind it. Instead it enjoyed the services of a more basic version of that device: a newly recruited youth of nineteen—myself.

The device we were using was a substantially built balance plough which carried two oppositely orientated ploughs mounted on the two arms of a wide splayed, V-shaped steel beam. My job was to control the appropriate plough's entry at the commencement of the furrow, trudge after it across the field and at the far end ease it out progressively until the share lay upon the head-land. Then, when the tractor had been backed up, I released the haulage shackle and while my uncle was circling round to reposition himself for the return journey swung the ponderous artifact over so that the opposite plough assumed the desired position after which I re-connected the shackle and set off on another cross-country walk.

I remember calculating, some time later, how far I shuffled and stumbled during the course of one of those days. Given that an acre comprises an area 220 yds. by 22 yds. and the plough turned a furrow of 9 inches width we made 88 traverses of the field per acre, and since 8 furlongs equal 1 mile it was evident that my feet covered 11 miles per acre, and we cultivated far in excess of 1 acre per day!

Work always continued until dusk. When we looked across the fields and saw a light in the cottage window we knew that the dinner table was being prepared and that it was time we were off—but not just like that, oh no! There was the tractor to be seen to first.

Contrary to the fairly common modern practice the machine was seldom taken back to the farmyard at the end of the day's work; unless the field we were occupied in was adjacent to the stackyard it was left on the headland. After all it was an extensive farm and many of the fields were a considerable distance from the farmstead and compared with today's models the tractor's speed of travel was of a very low order indeed. Ist. gear gave $2^1/_4$ mph; 2nd. gear gave 3 mph; 3rd gear gave $4^1/_2$ mph while reverse gear gave $2^5/_8$ mph. With these figures in mind the time spent in making the homeward and return journeys was regarded as time lost—time when the tractor could have been doing useful work. In view of this logic such journeys were never countenanced.

As I have already intimated, there was the tractor to be seen to before we could point our cycles in the direction of home. Given that there was the possibility of frost – and according to Sam there was always this danger after the clocks had been put back – the unalterable procedure was as follows. Uncouple the plough and drive onto the headland. Turn off the kerosine and turn on the gasoline allowing the engine to run for four or five minutes before stopping it. Drain the water from the engine and radiator (anti-freeze solutions were becoming available but we were never provided with any). Clean off the oil and dust from the engine. Remove compacted soil from between the rear wheel spuds. Cover engine and radiator with sack bags. Cover the cooling-water receptacle with more sack bags. Cover the driver's pressed steel seat with a sack bag and then, and not until then, we set off for home.

The first chore in the morning was the undoing of all we had done the night before. Then the thing had to be started. There was no self starter nor battery. Ignition was by means of a magneto fitted with an impulse starter. A hand-adjusted lever controlled the ignition 'advance' or 'retard' while the throttle or engine speed was under the control of a second manually positioned lever. To assist with starting on very cold days gasoline priming cups were fitted to the cylinder head.

I would stand at the ready by the starting handle while Sam would turn on the gasoline tap, adjust the ignition lever, (not too far advanced or the starting handle would kick back like a mule), position the throttle lever and in severe weather feed the priming cups with gasoline. Then I would crank the engine praying that it would start on the first or second attempt. Once started it would be allowed to warm up for four or five minutes before changing over from gasoline to kerosine.

After all these years I can still visualise these, often dismal, dark winter mornings on some remote headland with the wind blowing a gale from the North Sea or the rain beating a ceaseless tattoo on the engine hood. And often on the bleaker days I would almost weep with the agony of hotaches.

Although I often longed for the opportunity to drive the tractor such abysmal days inclined me to the opinion that the walking, however arduous, was far preferable to being seated behind the steering wheel taking the brunt of the wind, the rain, and the searing cold, (for the machine was not furnished with a cab). At least the exercise kept me warm.

When I watch a modern day tractor driver at work on one of the sophisticated breeds of machine with substantial cab, hydraulic actuated power take-off, self starter, rubber tyres, high road speeds and electric lighting, I murmur an old man's phrase, 'You don't know you're born'. But then I relent and surmise: 'But then, given the same equipment, I imagine you'd cope just as well as we did.'

TRANSPORT

FOR SIX AND A HALF DAYS of the week local journeys in and around the Marsh were mainly accomplished by one or other of two means—on foot or by cycle. Fortunately the terrain was highly suitable for the latter means of transport.

Residents who occasionally felt inclined to travel further afield had four opportunities to so indulge themselves. On Thursdays Tibbs' 'Ivy Coach' left from in front of Kent's blacksmith's shop at about mid morning en route for Kings Lynn and returned around tea time. On the same day, as an alternative, a second coach made the round trip to Spalding and back. Each Wednesday the same coach firm provided the villagers with an opportunity to visit the market in Boston.

Saturday, which saw the greatest migration of the St. Marks population to foreign parts, will be discussed later.

In view of the fact that the majority of able bodied men were at work on Tuesdays and Wednesdays the usual occupants of these green painted buses were housewives, single non-working females and a sprinkling of retired gentlemen.

On one occasion only did Fred and myself have the good fortune to enjoy one of these outings; the venue was Boston.

That morning fate was uncommonly kind; kind since it arranged for the rain to come bucketing down at 7.00 am—the time when our daily labours should have begun. Now by some unwritten law the order or precedence in finding employment for the workforce during such unfavourable weather conditions was as follows. Firstly married men living in the farmer's cottages; secondly married men living elsewhere and thirdly, if there were still jobs of an urgent nature to be carried out, single men living on the farm. That morning Mr. Tom Brown did not seem disposed to avail himself of our services. In no time at all we were dressed in our going out togs and off down the village to board the bus.

And what a delightful journey it turned out to be; sad it is that such experiences come but once in a lifetime. What an ambience of friendliness and jollity filled the confines of that small coach, and for once Time took a back seat.

No one, including the driver – especially the driver – seemed in any great hurry to reach our destination. If Mrs Bloggs was not at her usual picking point then, said our genial driver, we will wait until she arrives. 'Oh, she'll come,' he confided with an air of certainty, 'she'll come, she allus does.' And she did come and was helped up the steps and settled in her seat before the clutch was let in and we were off again.

We stopped at a gateway. Beyond ran a path to a distant cottage. 'She's laate to-daay is owd Alice,' ventured one old gentleman. The driver nodded. 'Go and give her a knock, she's happen over-slept.' And off went the Good Samaritan and met the lady coming out of her door and locked the door for her, took her shopping bag and lent her his arm as he escorted her to the bus.

What we did in Boston besides looking at the Stump, wolfing down some fish and chips and watching for awhile the antics at the cattle market I can no longer recall. Perhaps we just did nothing and sometimes that can be one of life's sublime pleasures.

At the time appointed we made for the bus. It was parked in the market place adjacent to an inn. Apart from the driver, who seemed totally unconcerned, no other person was present. 'Perhaps they are in the pubs,' was his conclusion. 'Why don't you join them, and don't worry about the time—we shan't leave without you.'

Eventually all the passengers returned loaded with their purchases. A rail running around the edge of the coach's roof formed a kind of roof rack within the confines of which the more bulky items were stacked. A man standing on the top of a short access ladder received these items as they were passed up to him and arranged them to the best advantage.

Above one curious Bostonian paused to view the loaded

coach as it stood in readiness for the return journey; it merited the attention. Both the market and the shops had been scoured for an unbelievable variety of household requisites. I recall seeing perched on top a zinc dolly tub; a rubbing board; a set of dollies, two or three besoms; a bathtub; a roll of wire netting; a crate of flustered chickens and other like essentials.

Inside the ladies clung to their overful shopping bags or nursed on their knees mysterious parcels wrapped in brown paper and tied with string. As light relief a diminutive piglet scampered up and down resisting all attempts to capture it.

On the homeward voyage several of the menfolk lit their pipes or Woodbines and filled the already stuffy interior with wraithes of acrid blue smoke. Yet scarce a lady wrinkled a nose in distaste or wafted a hand as a sign of reproof. Stout Linconshire ladies indeed; if not of body then assuredly of heart.

So we jogged and rumbled homeward, stopping at this road and that to retrieve some artifact from the roof rack and to see it and its owner safely set on the last leg of her journey.

Lincolnshire Road Cars don't run a service like that!

Then there was Saturday, the day of the Marsh folk's general exodus. The day, or rather afternoon when, after a week of toil the bustling pleasant town of Holbeach beckoned. The young men, fit and vigourous, took to their cycles heading for the Hippodrome, the Crown, the String of Horses, the gastronomic delights of the fish and chip shop on the Boston road, or an exploratory stroll along the High Street to eye and hopefully chat up the lasses. While they thus disported themselves their cycles were conveniently stored in the yard of the String of Horses. But if you eschewed the bicycle there were two choices of motorised transport available, the Ivy and the one which I used regularly until I acquired my first two wheeler, Tegerdines's all-purpose vehicle.

My landlady had informed me that I would catch this latter bus outside the village Post Office so it was there that I stood that long ago Saturday afternoon in the conpany of other would-be travellers. From time to time one or other of them would scan the horizon for signs of its approach—in land as flat as that the horizon was the only limit to one's range of vision. When someone cried: 'Here it comes,' I drew a handful of coins from my pocket in readiness for boarding. When the vehicle which ultimately appeared round Farrow's corner turned out to be a lorry I mentally questioned the local's powers of observation.

They were right of course as I was soon to discover. Within a short space of time the lorry bottom was swept clean of the debris resulting from the recent hauling of a load of potatoes, a tarpaulin cover was dropped over the body and benches placed in position—Tegardine's one hourly service to Holbeach was ready to commence operations. Thus I made my first excursion to that pleasant country town; many more were to follow.

With the potential for trade which St. Marks and the other Marsh villages offered it was inevitable that other concerns would enter into competition with the village shops, consequently transport devoted to the carrying of household goods and chattels rather than people was to be seen wending its way along the quiet roads. Rounds were established which reularly served the several hamlets and villages; nor did these assiduous and enterprising tradesmen neglect to call on the many remote and often isolated cottages in the area.

The names of three of these spring to mind. On Monday Jim Holland called with horse and covered cart; he dealt in groceries and was an employee of the firm of Curtis whose shop was in Holbeach. A second weekly visitor was a representative of Redding and Son; his stock in trade was hardware and paraffin and he solicited trade on Tuesdays. For those in need of vegetables, fruit and tinned goods there was always Mr. Starr who obliged with his presence on Fridays—but not with a horse and cart; he had a van!

11. St. Mark's Church. On the side of the village 'street' opposite to the dyke.

ENTERTAINMENT

WHEN IT CAME TO the provision of entertainment, recreation and out of work diversion, St. Mark's was no better nor worse than the majority of English villages. Cinemas were already a well established form of escapism and were usually to be found in even the smallest towns, but although there were a few villages scattered around the country which enjoyed the weekly visit of some peripatetic film exhibitor, St. Marks was not one of them.

The nearest venue where the 'star struck' could enjoy the antics of Laurel and Hardy or the vivacity of the newly discovered Jessie Matthews was the Hippodrome in Holbeach. When I arrived it was a comparitively new venture having been opened in 1929.

Before the advent of the silver screen the older generation, had, like their counterparts in many other small rural communities, been content with the simpler pleasures. And so they continued, the lives of the not so young moving with the same unalterable rhythm, the same unhurried tempo as of old. An evening around the fireside with their families was all that some aspired to; others habitually sought the company of old friends and companions in one or other of the two inns. Not a few were still finding inspiration and assurance in the Church and joining wholeheartedly in its various functions, especially the splendid garden parties organised as fund raising ventures. My Uncle Sam was prominent in this latter activity of church attendance. Being the organist his services were in constant demand for the Sunday services, choir practices, and other musical events. These duties he performed with a sense of dedication and commitment but on such evenings as he was free he welcomed the opportunity of joining with his wife and children in that little lamp-lit room I remember so vividly.

But the young were not so easily satisfied. The Church did not draw them as it had done their fathers and grandfathers.

There was of course the recreation field and in the winter months a group of youths could be seen enjoying an al fresco game of football on Saturday afternoons; early dusk curtailed such sport in the evenings. During summer this gave way to cricket. One fixture eagerly enjoyed by a vociferous and partisan crowd of residents of all ages was the one when the married men challenged the single men. Sam, who was an excellent player, and the Rev. Browne-Wilkinson who had played for his university, were regarded as the backbone of their side. How eagerly the unmarried among the spectators awaited their downfall; with what cries of jubilation would they greet such an enventuality.

Afterwards victors and vanquished sat down to a hearty repast in the recreation room followed by an impromptu concert, the enjoyment of which was shared by many of the spectators. Some said the losers paid for the meal but I was never able to verify this.

What is certain is that to me it was the very epitome of village life as I had often imagined it.

In general however I felt that the young at heart were beginning to feel circumscribed, constricted by their environs. More and more they were becoming aware of another world beyond the village and with growing impatience wanted to participate in the new experiences it had to offer. That I think was why Holbeach, Spalding, Kings Lynn, and Boston proved so irresistible to them on those long ago Saturday afernoons. Many, I believe, were restless without having any clear idea of the real cause. The war which was soon to take many of them to distant towns and far away lands helped to crystalise their incipient desires; after the conflict was over several of the youths I had known in those days were never able to settle down in their old occupations and departed for pastures new. The Yanks expressed it quite succinctly in the song:

How're you goin' to keep them down on the farm
now that they've seen Marie?

As for myself during the few months following my arrival the evenings were spent with my uncle and his family except for the occasional game of football on the recreation ground and the increasing visits to Holbeach. On these occasions I was always accompanied by my friend Fred and seldom failed to end the evening with a visit to the Hippodrome.

Yet the evenings in that little cottage living room were far from mundane; with three high spirited young girls to tease and torment me - good-humouredly of course - how could they be? Their mother was never slow to reprimand them if she considered their antics a little too boisterous, but my assurances that I really quite enjoyed it all seemed to allay her concern.

But how can I forget that other diversion with which Sam and myself whiled away many of those evenings—that new fangled thing called wireless? For those were the days of 2LO, of shops selling components and kits and high tension batteries, grid bias batteries, accumulators, headphones, and Brownie horn loudspeakers. The days of Build Your Own was upon us— ong before D.I.Y. had entered the language. And we, like many thousands more, had caught the bug.

Sam's younger brother, who still lived in Stalybridge, would from time to time send him a bundle of old wireless magazines, an event which caused Eva to sigh and shake her head with an air of resignation. For my uncle, after carefully scrutinising the well thumbed pages would invariably come across a new revolutionary circuit which promised better selectivity, improved reception, more powerful output or some other more desirable property. The existing set was forthwith doomed.

His wife knew there would be no listening that night; no music hall from Birkenhead with the young and coming Donald Peers to entertain her. So the knitting needles would go into top gear and she would, from time to time, glance at the table with an expression of dour resignation.

Not that my uncle seemed to notice these signs of incipient rebellion; like most enthusiasts he seemed to imagine that everyone else was as engrossed as he was. Down would come the receiver from its place of honour on the copper and soon there would scarcely be room for a tea-cup on that table top. From the disembowelled set lay strewn condensers, fixed and variable; valves; resistors; plug-in coils, and inumerable lengths of vari-coloured rubber insulated wire.

Often the good lady retired to bed leaving us to our labours — the children had been ushered off some time previously. How often we worked until close on midnight in order to complete the construction only to find the results scarcely an improvement on those obtained from the receiver recently dismantled. I never can, nor do I wish, to forget those nights.

CHAPEL

MY UNCLE WAS A DEVOUT SERVANT of his church. In St. Mark's churchyard there is a simple stone which records that Sam was organist in the church for twenty-five years; it was a labour of love.

Church of England services had never attracted me. I loved singing but that denomination seemed to frown on any form of vocal enthusiasm. Raising one's voice above pianissimo bordered on a misdemeanour or at least an exhibition of bad taste. As for the psalms—well I never did manage to fit the tune to the words.

In the beginning I did accompany Sam to the services on Sunday evenings mainly because it appeared to please him. But my antipathy was never diminished thereby and secretly I felt somewhat hypocritical.

It was a chance meeting with a young man on the recreation ground during a game of football which led to my introduction to the chapel in Holbeach Bank. He and his family — mother, father, brothers Bill, Ron, and Eric and his sister Elizabeth were regular worshippers there. After my first visit in response to their invitation I too became a habitual attender. The welcome I received and the sense of genuine fellowship I experienced motivated me to persuade Fred that a visit might be well worth the effort. He not only discovered the same sense of fulfilment but also met the girl he later married.

But there was more to that place of worship than the Sunday services. During the winter months a series of visits to outlying chapels was arranged, the intention of which was to entertain the host congregation; and how well we succeeded!

Being totally unfamiliar with the surrounding countryside those dark evening bus jaunts always seemed infused with an aura of unreality. Even if you wiped off the obscuring mist from the windows nothing could be seen except the short stretch of road illuminated by the head lights. Nothing else could be discerned except an all-enveloping darkness for the roads were totally without any kind of lighting. They were like journeys across a vast uncharted ocean.

What was the entertainment we provided? Sometimes it took the format of a Service of Song. Various members of the party would take it in turns to read the chapters of a story and at appropriate points soloists would sing a relevant hymn or sacred song. In view of the nature of the premises secular songs were not considered suitable although a point could be stretched in the case of such offerings as 'Bless this House' or 'The Lost Chord'

On other occasions we might present a concert; the same conditions concerning the contents still obtained. Whatever form the entertainment took the evening always ended up with a splendid supper provided by the host; a meal which reflected the hours that some of the ladies had spent in baking, cooking, and other necessary preparations.

As a matter of course the members of these other chapels would pay us a reciprocal visit when we would return their hospitality. Although Fred and I did no baking we could always be found in the little side room up to our elbows in soapsuds, cups, saucers and plates.

The Sunday School sermons, events in which the children were the chief participants, were held annually and drew enthusiastic audiences to the performances. The weeks beforehand were filled with much activity. There were new hymns for the children to learn while Fred, Madge (his wife-to-be) and myself, together with other members of the small but resolute choir, attempted to master some anthem or a not too ambitious choral extravaganza.

But it was the children's day really. What 'oh's' and 'ah's' of admiration the youngsters drew from the assembled crowd; the girls in their bright new frocks and gay colourful hair ribbons and the boys looking quite like little gentlemen in their new suits and plastered-down hair. What a sacrifice of much of their meagre and hard earned income many of the parents must have made to ensure that that day would be a very, very special one for their offspring.

Nor must I omit to mention the annual chapel outing. Run especially for the benefit of the children, it gave them a taste of sea, sand, and all the fun of the fair in the days when annual holidays were virtually non-existant— at least down the Marsh. Skegness was the usual venue and there was never a shortage of willing helpers to supervise and care for the ebullient youngsters. A tea was always laid on in a large cafe on the corner of Scarborough Avenue after which the delights of the

12. The author on the Chapel outing 1933

seaside were there for the lads and lassies to explore.

Nor were some of the grown-ups slow to extract the utmost enjoyment from the day. There were cups of tea, ice cream, fish and chips and still more tea and then, as if the surfeit of sea air had released some hitherto masochistic tendencies this gastronomic extravaganza would inevitably lead to a visit to the Pleasure Beach. It did not take long to persuade most of them that fish and chips and madly whirling roundabouts were not compatible — not compatible at all.

The older and obviously wiser element contented themselves with a gentle stroll to some convenient promenade bench from which they watched the passing throng and, as they put it, 'let their dinner go down'.

But that day like all enjoyable days had to come to an end and all too soon the bus was bearing its tired but happy contingent back to the distant Marsh. There was singing at first but as the miles rolled by it petered out. Lulled by the motion of the vehicle heads lolled and many fell into an untroubled sleep.

Yet once we arrived at the market place in Boston the young men and women clamoured for the driver to stop outside

13. Chapel outing—Skegness 1933.
The author on the left.

the fish and chip saloon; there were stomachs not yet fully satisfied. From there to Fosdyke the stuffy interior of the coach reeked with the unmistakable odour of vinegar soaked chips.

As they reached their destination the little ones were carried off flushed, rumpled, and dead to the world. The latest song of the day which Kitty Masters was warbling might have been written for the occasion; it's title?

Little man you've had busy day.

14. And some went into service.

A Strange Meeting

THAT FRIENDLY, EBULLIENT YOUTH Frank Haresign who had introduced me to his family and to the Holbeach Bank Chapel was responsible, a little later, for my meeting with one of the more unconventional characters to be found in the marshlands of the Wash.

I remember how one evening he invited me to take a cycle ride with him with the object of looking up an old friend; I didn't need asking twice!

His promise of a surprise was no exaggeration.

We left the village of St. Marks by the road which leads towards Fosdyke Bridge. It was new territory to me at the time but later I travelled that same route many times on my way to spear dabs on the bed of the Welland just east of that bridge.

On that balmy evening of long ago with legs imbued with the energy and enthusiasm of youth it was not long before we reached the isolated inn which went under the name of The Hare and Hounds.

Here my companion dismounted and I assumed that we had reached our journey's end. I was wrong; our objective could scarcely have been more different! Frank leaned his cycle against the wall of the hostelry, signalled me to do likewise and then crossed to the opposite side of the deserted road. And he pointed; pointed over the seemingly endless stretch of mud, tangled seaweed, and small armies of foraging diminutive brown-green crabs.

And I too looked in the direction indicated and wondered whether what I saw was a mirage or reality. But it was real all right. There, standing upright in the alien sea of mud was a boat! A sailing vessel marooned and motionless, secured port and starboard by taut steel guylines upon which were threaded biscuit tin lids to thwart the would be invading long tailed rats.

It was not long before we were installed in the warm, comfortable cabin and enjoying the hot strong tea which the boat's owner had pressed upon us as a mark of his pleasure at our unexpected and plainly welcomed visit. For it was indeed a lonely place for a man to inhabit by himself.

I must have sat for an hour or more listening while the old man related something of his strange and unusual lifestyle.

What I gathered and remember from that weather tanned man of the sea and from the memory jogging reminders made to me recently by Frank, my companion on that distant evening – yes Frank is still alive and I communicated with him quite recently – is broadly as follows.

15. *The author and Frank Haresign aboard* the Marytrue. *[Registered at Lynn].*

The man with the bluff voice, dark blue roll-neck sweater, and the peaked hat was Skipper Parsons. (We never did ascertain his real given name.) Years before he had sailed a barge along the Holbeach Creek which ran from the River Welland to a spot close by where his boat now stood. To enable this journey to be made the sea wall had been furnished with a sluice. Hence that end of the creek became known as Sluice End and the inland termination as Holbeach Creek End.

The purpose of these journeys was to carry shingle for the use of the Holbeach Council who used it for the repair of roads under their jurisdiction.

But the time eventually arrived when he decided he had seen enough shingle to last him a lifetime (and a bit more!) so he bought himself a sailing boat, moored it at Snettisham not too far from New Hunstanton, and spent his summers taking out parties of fishermen.

As soon as the season was over however he returned to his haunts, crossed the Wash, turned into the Welland, beat it up the old familiar Holbeach Creek and moored where we had found him.

Frank was unable to tell me where he had gone from there. About the boat itself my old friend was more informative. A year or so after I had left the district there came an exceptionally high tide which engulfed old Skips pride and joy; this co-incided with one of the worst freeze-ups that the area had seen for many a year. The vessel became immobilized, encased in a cold shroud of ice until, shortly afterwards, during a violent storm, it was unceremoniously ripped in half, the seaward section being borne out to sea while the other section remained the helpless butt of wind, rain, and tide until it was as if it had never been.

The Weaker Sex

WITHIN THE AREA OF THE MARSH farm labouring was the only occupation open to the men-folk. My preoccupation with this concept has almost led me into an unpardonable sin of omission— that of failing to give some account of the rôle that the women, particularly the married ones with young families, played in the day to day tasks on the farms.

It was to be expected that girls and unmarried women would go out to work much as their sisters did in the towns and cities; all that differed was the nature of the employment. Instead of factories, offices and shops their main centre of activity lay on the land. There was some scope as shop assistants in Holbeach but understandably, in view of the lack of transport, the prospect of cycling the not inconsiderable distance morning and night in all weathers was not particularly appealing. A few went into service in the large houses but this did not significantly dent the available labour force.

Although there were few tasks to which they could not turn their hands the bulb fields seemed to be their special domain; at setting bulbs, flower pulling, nobbing, lifting, cleaning and sorting the bulbs they were well nigh indispensable.

Watching them thus occupied was one of the outstanding recollections of my sojourn at Willow Tree. I swear that no other body of people can make as much noise and seemingly so enjoy themselves as a gang of Lincolnshire lasses in a bulb field and yet amid all the apparent pandemonium carry out their tasks with such commendable efficiency.

Yet marriage and the advent of children did not necessarily signal a transposition from the sphere of gainful employment to the exclusive dual rôle of housewife and mother— at least not when the offspring were of school age. Then it was that the Marsh housewife was seen at her industrious best. First thing in the morning while the family were at breakfast she would busy herself with the preparation of lunches for her husband and children; the youngsters ate their midday meal at school and father took his out in the field. Except for weekends seldom was the lunch enjoyed indoors during the summer months.

Once her spouse had gone off to his work and her dependent brood's dress and general appearance been scrutinised and approved, and even before their departing, scampering footsteps were out of earshot, the assiduous lady was making ready for the main meal of the day; this was always enjoyed in the evening. There were potatoes to be peeled, additional vegetables to be prepared, the popular and filling suet pudding to be made and these, together probably with an appropriate cut of boiling bacon, would be placed in a three tiered steamer in readiness for their eventual cooking.

Even then her labours were not over. There were pots to be washed, the coconut matting to be taken up and shaken, and maybe the stone floor to be scrubbed and the beds to be made. Then, when her critical eye was satisfied with the general appearance of her domain the house would be locked up before she departed for her job on the farm.

Later in the afternoon she would return to cook the meal in readiness for her family's return when they would all sit around the table to enjoy the results of her culinary skill.

Such a catalogue of chores! How, I often wondered, did she find the time to do the washing, clean the windows and so forth? The mending was reserved for later in the evening.

Yet it was not just pin money that the women were striving for; without the extra money they earned many real necessities would not have been forthcoming.

CHILDREN

HOW COULD ONE FORGET the contribution made by the children? I recall first seeing them at work in the field known as the Big Rabbit bank. We were singling sugar beet and they joined us after school, scrambling about on their knees and doing the singling while we concentrated on the chopping out. Several of the labourers wives joined us also. Although they received no payment from the farmer for their efforts such assistance helped the menfolk to get over the ground much faster and since they were paid at piece rate this helped to supplement their earnings.

Adverse weather conditions delaying the gathering in of the harvest could well lead to the involvement of the village school's older pupils. Several of the area's more important and influential farmers were on that school's Board of Governors and at times of such crises could present to that body a reasonable case for granting such pupils a break from their lessons so that they might work on the farms when the elements became more propitious.

Doubtless the youngsters were pleased on two counts; firstly they escaped for a time the rigours of the classroom and secondly the few shillings they earned (this time they were on the payroll!) provided them with the wherewithall for a rare spending bonanza!

THE LIGHTER SIDE

WHEN I FIRST MET Mr. Tom Brown the farm foreman I was convinced that for his idiosyncracies of dress, habits and mannerisms he was the most outstanding 'character' I had met—or was likely to meet. Later I was to become acquainted with a labourer whose outlandish behaviour made Tom seem almost ordinary by comparison.

This latter person bore the name of Fred Wileman but more usually he answered to the nickname of 'Porky'. Some of the escapades he had indulged in before my arrival were told to me by Sam, sometimes as we sat around the fire, or during the morning lunch breaks. Had I not been convinced of my uncle's veracity some of these tales I would have discounted as mere fabrications, so unlikely were they. Such incidents as I later personally observed however inclined me to the opinion that Sam had been under, rather than over, flamboyant in his narrations.

There was for instance the story of the bicycle.

Now Porky sometimes came to work on a bicycle but more usually he came with a bicycle; the distinction is important. 'Coming with' meant pushing or walking but certainly not riding. That machine of his was a kind of mechanical malingerer patently determined never to carry out the function for which it was originally purchased.

One morning a broken chain would prevent its being ridden; the next a puncture would serve the same purpose. On another occasion the handlebars came loose robbing its rider of the ability to steer in the desired direction.

Still the persistent Porky arrived each morning with the recalcitrant artifact—until one memorable Saturday. Then we saw approaching from the direction of Willow Tree what was at first believed to be an apparition but which as it drew closer proved to be Porky astride a brand new cycle resplendent with nickel plate, shiny green enamel, and a Sturmy Archer three speed gear. He was off, he said, come the afternoon, to visit some relative who lived out Boston way and was resolved to make the journey in style on a machine of proven reliability. We all applauded his foresight and wished him a pleasant trip.

It is not difficult to imagine our surprise when, on the following Monday morning, he arrived pushing his former cycle as of old. At first he was morose and uncommunicative; not until we sat down to take our morning break did he satisfy our eager curiosity.

'New bike,' he growled between mouthfuls of bread and boiled bacon, 'It wur no better nor the owd un. Hafeway back it had a puncture an' the chain come off an' ah cudna get it on.'

'So what did you do?' ventured somebody.

The aggrieved one wiped his mouth with the back of his hand before grunting, 'Why ah chucked it over the hedge an' come back on the bus.'

Now how many folks do you know who would have, could have, done that?

Nor must his confrontation with the foreman be forgotten. It was a Monday morning when he was sent to paint a gate and the short length of abutting fence. After a Sunday night in the New Inn, Monday morning wasn't his best day; until midday talking just wasn't on the agenda.

Tom rolled up in his trap round about nine, said 'Whoa' to his mare and 'Mornin' to Porky. Ignoring him Porky kept slapping on the paint. The moustache adorned face beneath the black hat adopted a peeved expression; its owner decided to abandon the benign approach and adopt a more officious one.

"A' you got enough paint theer to finish the job?' he queried brusquely.

The painter-for-the-time-being paused at the end of a brush stroke, turned and contemplated the pony trap and its rider as if making some mental calculation and then proclaimed: 'Tom, ah reckon awv'e enough paint left to paint the gate, the fence, the trap, the horse an' thee as well if thar't still here in two minutes from now.'

'Gee up,' said Tom and left at a quick trot.

Only a man like Porky could have got away with it.

16. 'Ha' you got enough paint, Porky?'

CELEBRATION

In the town of my birth dancing was a well established form of recreation with a wide range of venues. The dedicated devotees of the art would flock to the sumptuous Palais de Dance, while the group of youths of which I was a member were satisfied with the sixpenny Saturday night hops in some church hall or Constitutional Club. Yet during all my time down the Marsh I attended only one dance and that because it was held on a very special occasion—the day set apart to celebrate the silver jubilee of King George V and Queen Mary.

The leading members of the Holbeach Bank community had decided that a concert followed by a dance would provide a fitting climax to the day's festivities and I, being now an habitue of that village, was invited to assist in the organisation of the affair.

The concert was an unqualified success. The Haresigns, that family which had first introduced me to the Bank Chapel, contributed piano solos by the daughter and accordion pieces by the father. I sang a couple of songs and played a popular song or two on my mouth-organ. A gratifyingly sizeable number of the local residents were persuaded to overcome their normally shy dispositions and present their favourite pieces; they needn't have suffered any apprehension about their reception. Each and every act, good, bad or indifferent was greeted with the same rapturous applause. It was the kind of night when laughter came easily. Many of the menfolk had previously paid a visit to the local hostelry and were mellow to the point of being maudlin. Save for one old codger 'Encore' came readily to their lips; that worthy cried 'Encore be damned, let t'same bloke sing again.'

But it is the ensuing dance that is burned deep in my memory. The band was a two man ensemble— Mr. Haresign on the accordion and myself on the mouth organ. For some reason beyond our comprehension two tunes of the day took and held the dancers' fancy— *Oh play To Me Gypsy* and *Dancing With My Shadow*. No matter how many times we played them they were still repeatedly requested. My mouth was sore and my companion nodding off to sleep when the time came for the last waltz and the National Anthem.

That was one of the very rare occasions when my close friend Fred was conspicuous by his absence; but it was a balmy night and he was courting and two people in love can find more interesting things to do than dance.

I did not know it then but that dance marked the beginning of the end; my stay down the Marsh was drawing to a close.

LEAVING

MY LEAVING WAS NOT A PREMEDITATED ACTION. The day started seemingly like any other day— and then I was sent hay-tedding. This wasn't one of my better skills. Given practice I suppose I could have become tolerably proficient at it but since the opportunity to practice only came once a year that could have taken some time. By mid-morning I had fallen well behind the rest of the gang despite my most strenuous and unremitting efforts; then Tom Brown arrived. He was at his irascible worst and gave me a telling-off which, in his opinion, was well deserved. All my protestations about effort and intent buttered no parsnips as far as he was concerned; in the heat of the moment I precipitately announced my intention to quit. The foreman showed no inclination to persuade me differently— so that was that.

As I walked off the field I was smouldering with injured pride and trying to distance myself from any blame in the matter. Yet in my heart of hearts I knew that my self-esteem was bruised because of my abject failure to match the efforts of my companions.

Yet surprisingly, with each step I took away from that swathe-covered field, the realisation grew that I was really leaving an occupation that suited neither my temperament nor inclination. How long this belief had been buried in my subconcious I couldn't tell — what I did begin to acknowledge was that Tom was not at fault; unwittingly he had been the catalyst that brought it to the surface. Now as the cottage at Willow Tree grew nearer my new-found elation grew all the greater.

Unlike Fred I had formed no association with any particular female and this lack of attachment meant I was not provisionally bound, as it were, to the celebration of some future nuptials and the almost certain concomitant of a future committed to things rustic.

In truth, occasionally and fleetingly, the thought had crossed my mind of what I might do if some lass and I came to the point of contemplating marriage, but in my lackadaisical manner this theoretical eventuality had been left in the lap of the Gods. Now for better or worse the decision had been taken and the prospects of returning to a way of life more suited to my aspirations lightened my steps and put a song on my lips.

When Sam was aquainted with the facts that evening he was both perturbed and concerned; he even offered to intercede with Mr. Bowser on my behalf in an endeavour to get me reinstated, but I assured him there was no way I was prepared to prolong my stay down the Marsh for a moment longer than was necessary. The idyll was over. There is a curious tailpiece to this story. When I saw Fred at the Bank chapel later that evening I was astounded to learn that he too had handed in his notice that very same day without knowing anything at all about my decision.

We both left the village together a day or two later, cycling to what we thought would be a new life, a different life filled with all sorts of exciting possibilities. It didn't quite turn out like that. When we reached Stamford Fred decided to turn back. It wasn't a decision taken lightly; the last thing he wanted to do was offend me. But I knew he had left the love of his life behind and needed to be with her so, after wishing each other 'bon voyage!' we went our separate ways.

Fred found employment with a different farmer, I had a stroke of luck, almost immediately securing a position with Messrs. Cooch & Son of Northampton. This family firm specialised in agricultural engineering and there, among other things, I found myself fitting and erecting potato riddling and sorting machines.

Conclusion

Up until the outbreak of the war I paid many visits to that remote village. The welcome was always cordial and few there were who didn't remember the two odd characters who had burst upon them like meteors and departed just as suddenly. It was not to be wondered at; neither before nor since had they nor have they been treated to the spectacle of Fred riding his green Hopper bicycle backwards through the village with me following behind rendering selections on my mouth organ.

But my sojourn there taught me much. I felt privileged to have been so generously and warmly welcomed, stranger that I was, and I felt chastened to have rubbed shoulders with a people so patient and unassuming. I rejoiced at their impish wit and more than anything else appreciated deeply the rough compassion they showed when they laughed with me rather than at me as I struggled, more often than not unsuccessfully, to master the age-old skills that fell so readily to their calloused hands.

Ever since those memorable years I have never permitted myself to refer to those who toil on the land as 'labourers'— nor yet allowed to go unchallenged the assertions of those who did. What I did observe, and prove by my attempted emulation, was a measure of skill and expertise equalling, and often surpassing, that displayed by those in other so-called more prestigious occupations. Someday perhaps they will get their just desserts — but not until the eyes of the nation are unblinkered and can see and realise that food production is as vital, if not more so, as turning out motor cars and washing machines.

And finally a long held personal aberration of mine for which many may chide me but which I shall always cherish. Lincolnshire is a many-acred shire with a topography as diverse as that of many other English shires. But mention Lincolnshire to me and my mind conjures up a picture, a vista stretching from Spalding in the west to the shore of the Wash in the east; from Sutton Bridge to the south and northwards to Boston. That is my own private, personal remembered domain.

The bridge over the Welland by which one left Spalding for the Holbeach road was the gateway by which I first entered my new life; no other part of Lincolnshire ever evokes such nostalgia as that expanse of interminable flatness. As flat as a carpet and coloured more vividly and variously than the most exotic Persian wall drapes; a patchwork of Nature's unsurpassable hues. A palette of yellows; oats, barley and wheat shading from pale sunkissed straw to rich wind swept gold. The rich dark green of potato fields; the glossier green of sugar beet bejewelled with sparking raindrops; the umber and sienna of fresh ploughed earth and the vivid, breathtaking slashes of colour when the silk and velvet blooms of daffodils and tulips marched like colourful battalions from headland to distant headland. That is, and always will be, my Lincolnshire.

But oh, Willow Tree! Willow Tree! Amid all your profusion of earth's bounties; amid your wheat and oats, your potatoes and cabbages, your cauliflower and sugar beet, amid all that flourished on your broad and fertile acres there was not to be found, on one or any morning, the wherewithall to render more palatable that first welcome cup of tea. There was no milk!